MW01241234

Second Chance

A Journey of Hope and Healing

Helen Kniepmann

Inspiring Voices®
A Service of **Guideposts**

Inspiring Voices books may be ordered through booksellers or by contacting:

Inspiring Voices
1663 Liberty Drive
Bloomington, IN 47403
www.inspiringvoices.com
1 (866) 697-5313

Bible quotes from: New American Bible, St Joseph Edition
Copyright 1991, 1986, l970 by the Confraternity of Christian Doctrine.

ISBN: 978-1-4624-0942-6 (sc)

Printed in the United States of America.

Inspiring Voices rev. date: 06/17/2014

⌒∶ Contents ∶⌒

⌣⋮ DEDICATION ⋮⌣

This book is dedicated to my family who were so loving, helpful and supportive throughout the journey I took from the uncertainty of Stage IV cancer to the jubilation of recovery. They gave me encouragement to accept the new challenges I faced every day. They have always been there for me, no matter time, cost or event.

During the weeks that I was critically ill, they traveled from out of town numerous times to sit by my bed, pray and do whatever needed to be done. My son, Mark, and his family, who live nearby, were on call 24/7 and available at a moment's notice.

What an awesome family God has given me. They are the best.

∽ FOREWORD ∾

I first met Helen when she was in the middle of her battle with cancer. Her son Ken, a good friend of mine and now the Executive Director of our ministry, asked a small group of us to pray for her healing. We added our prayers to those of the many others who love her, wanted her to live, and believed Jesus could heal her.

Praying for healing, whether for one self or for someone you love, is always a vulnerable experience. It requires each of us to let go of our control and trust in a God we cannot apprehend with our senses. We have to believe and hope, and this is never easy especially when our very life is dependent upon it. Prayer for healing involves faith, hope, and love—three qualities that I saw in Helen when I met her.

Helen's faith is strong, but it did not come easily or all at once. It grew over time as she faced each of the many challenges that came her way. As you will read in the pages to follow, her faith was put to the test, time and again. At some of those times, she began to lose hope, but just as it was being snuffed out, the Holy Spirit brought it back again, stronger than ever.

Hope is always critical in our lives, but it is especially challenged when facing the ominous fear and hopelessness of stage IV cancer. What do you hope for? As a Christian who believes deeply in the reality of heaven, Helen hoped for the ultimate joy of being with Jesus. But she was not ready to die, nor did she believe it was time for her to go. With many reasons to continue living, she set her hopes on being healed.

Her desire to live was fueled by her love for life and especially her love for family and friends. Most of all she loves God and wants to continue to serve him while on earth. I have had the privilege in recent years of seeing her love in action. Throughout this entire process, it seems it has grown stronger. I have personally witnessed incidents of this growth in love between her and her son Ken. What a beautiful thing to behold!

Faith, Hope, and Love are also essential for those who pray for healing. We believe in Jesus who said "Ask and you will receive." He assured us that we could do even greater works than he did. We keep our hopes fixed on heaven, knowing that ultimately, we will not be disappointed. With hope, even death is a victory. Finally, and most importantly healing is an expression of love—both God's love and ours-reaching out to the suffering one, desiring the good for that person.

After many years of praying for healing, I have come to rest in this: when love is present, healing is always occurring. *God's love always heals.* The healing can be physical, emotional, or spiritual, but the ones we pray for are always healed in some way. For Helen, her healing went well beyond the elimination of the cancer in her body.

Through the process of battling stage IV cancer, the God who loves her deeply, also healed her body, soul, and spirit. May His glory be revealed to you as you read Helen's beautiful and uplifting story.

Bob Schuchts, Ph.D.
Author of ***Be Healed***
*Founder of **JPII Healing Center***

ᘇ᛬ PREFACE ᛬ᘈ

Life's journey takes us in many directions, and we never really know where or how it will end. It may be happy and enjoyable, or at times, disappointing, difficult and challenging. But, if we let God be our guide, it will be a good trip.

In July 2006, my day began by going to the clinic for my annual mammogram. My day ended with a "possible cancer" diagnosis. No one is ever prepared to hear those words, and I certainly was not. It changed my life and started me on a journey filled with many challenges and a deepening of faith. My life would never be the same again.

Worry could accomplish nothing. Saint Pio said "Worry is a lack of trust in God." I have a plaque on my nightstand that says "Before you go to bed at night give your troubles to God, He will be up all night anyway." How true. He is always there for us. I thank God for blessing me with the strength and faith to deal with all the difficulties and challenges of a Stage IV cancer diagnosis. It took some time to acquire this faith and trust. While I was praying and asking for total healing, I felt no matter what happened, I would be able to accept it.

I believe that cancer and cancer treatments are not between doctor and patient, but between doctor, patient and God. Leaving God out of the equation is like building a house without a foundation. A house without a good foundation will have nothing but problems and will collapse. God is the foundation that gave me strength to fight the disease, and faith to face the difficult days ahead.

I've been there, lived it, and survived. It is my hope that my story will help others to have courage and trust in God to see them through difficult times.

◡: Introduction :◠

Hearing a diagnosis of cancer is devastating. I was not prepared to hear those words and certainly not prepared to deal with it. However, after some time, I chose to accept it as a challenge and turn it over to God. This was too big for me, so I put it in His hands knowing He would take care of me, and He did.

The first days after the diagnosis of Stage IV cancer were very difficult and troubling. The days stretched into weeks, months, and then years.

With cancer we automatically think of chemo and its side effects. While we think of chemo as a cure, it is also a challenge. For some, it is a huge challenge, for others not quite that difficult. But, attitude always enters into this picture and it can make a huge difference in our response to treatment.

After going through many medical tests, chemo, radiation treatment, at one time being near death,

1

turning my life over to God, I received what most people call a miracle.

It took several weeks to accept what was happening and reach the point of total acceptance.

Through prayer, I reached the conclusion that I was going to eventually be cancer free. I just knew it was going to happen. It took six years to get there, but the words "your tests show no cancer present" were like music to my ears. I received a second chance at life.

∽ THE JOURNEY BEGINS ∾

Life is a journey. We do not control where it begins, but we can decide if we will enjoy the trip.

Growing up on a farm in southern Illinois during the depression years was not easy for my family. I was the youngest of five children in a Catholic family that many would describe as typical and average. We lived in a modest rural community. The church we attended was a small country church like those often pictured on Christmas cards. It was a quaint, white frame structure, with a steeple on the top of the roof, and located in a farming community referred to by the locals as "Beaver Prairie".

Despite this post-card image, my life was far from idyllic. Life in the post-depression years was hard in our rural community, and particularly hard on the farm. My childhood was surrounded by and sometimes involved in the hard work and chores required to keep the farm operating. While I always knew that my parents loved me, the harshness of life, combined with their "stoic" German roots, made for a childhood that was often long on work and short on play.

Beaver Prairie had a little one-room school that I attended for the first eight years of my education. Unless the weather was bad, we often walked two miles to school each day. We did not have electricity or any of the conveniences of modern life. (Yes, electricity had been invented by that time, I'm not that old. It's just that in the area we lived, the electric and phone lines had not yet been installed.) We did get electricity when I was about eleven years old.

I grew up without indoor plumbing or air conditioning. My bedroom was upstairs in our farmhouse. Neither the walls nor the ceiling were insulated, and we didn't have central heat. In the wintertime, we would run up the stairs and quickly hop in our beds. We had no trouble staying in our warm bed til morning.

We survived and I later realized what a great learning experience my life had been. Life isn't always easy, but it taught me how to hang in and not give up. We had what was really important, i.e., family, home, love and faith.

After grade school I attended a Catholic high school in a small town nearby, riding a bus for several hours each day. But, I didn't mind. I was just grateful that I could attend high school. This was one of my early challenges.

Walking into a school and classroom, knowing no one, is hard to do. Most of the students already had friends.

I didn't know a soul in the entire school other than my sister, and being accepted was not easy. That's when I learned the importance of perseverance. Over the years life became easier. Immediately after graduation I started working as a secretary and continued that occupation during my employment years. Life had already taught me that work and perseverance are necessary, and that things aren't always easy. Quitting certainly isn't acceptable and not an option.

I married my husband, Ray, in 1956 and moved from Illinois to St Louis County, MO. We raised our family of 4 (3 boys, 1 girl) sending them through the Catholic grade and high schools, and then college. We lived there 43 years before moving to Melbourne, FL where I presently live.

Faith, prayer and trust in God have always been a part of my life. I attended church and participated in parish activities. My faith had been passed down to me by my parents and for this I am grateful. However, I always felt the need for more, for growth in my faith life.

Our two older sons had moved to Melbourne, FL several years earlier and were involved in a church that was committed to increasing the faith of its parishioners. They were encouraging us to move to Florida when we retired. This would mean leaving some of our family behind and beginning a new life in a new place.

We had vacationed in Florida for a number of years, so we knew how beautiful it was. Since Ray did not like cold weather, he was eager to move to a warm climate. We were told "If you move to Florida you will always have visitors. Everyone loves to come to Florida." So, we eventually moved there. We said goodbye to our two youngest children, Kathy and Joe, along with their families, and many of our friends, and left our midwest life for Florida.

Once there, we became involved with our new parish and came to the conclusion that God brought us here for a reason. We knew that the people in our new community could help us grow in our faith. We felt so lucky and thankful. The weather was great,- we were surrounded by the beauty of Florida and had wonderful neighbors. Who could ask for more?

✎ Challenges and Diagnosis ✎

Cancer challenged my faith and propelled me on a journey filled with anxiety, uncertainty, and never knowing exactly what the next day might bring.

In July 2006 I had my yearly mammogram. I had a mammogram every year and previously had not had any problem, but this time it showed a suspicious spot in the breast and under the arm requiring a biopsy.

Sometimes, life can change in an instant. I went into the clinic thinking it would be routine, like all the other mammograms I had previously. Hearing there was a suspicious mass in the breast was so shocking, it was hard to absorb the problem I was facing. I walked out of the clinic with my husband, Ray, and told him I had a problem that needed further testing. It was only later that I finally realized this was really bad and concerning.

The biopsy results confirmed cancer, and the doctors immediately recommended a mastectomy. The mastectomy would require removing the breast and some lymph glands under the arm. Breast removal is very traumatic for many women, and I understand how deeply it can affect their sense of femininity and self-worth. Perhaps it was God's grace, or maybe just my practical German background, but it was not an emotional event for me. I just wanted to do what was necessary to free my body of the cancer. It was difficult though, as each successive test revealed more bad news.

My imagination was working overtime and though I had no official prognosis, I thought I only had 3 or 4 months to live. We humans seem to have a habit of thinking the worst and jumping to conclusions that are usually inaccurate. Fear was my constant companion.

As I think back, the time from first diagnosis to start of treatment seemed to be a most difficult period. Yes, the treatments were difficult, but by then I knew what was happening. For me, the early diagnosis stage was the most difficult. There were so many unanswered questions, so few answers, and so much uncertainty.

I have a wonderful neighbor, Merle, who offered to drive me to one of my early tests, a biopsy. I thought the test was not going to be a big deal and that I would not get any test results, so I accepted her offer. To my surprise, however, the doctor spoke to her and my husband giving them bad news about the biopsy. When I found out later that she had to hear the report from the doctor, I really felt bad. I didn't want her to be in the midst of all my troubles.

Merle was a great friend in that difficult moment and she has continued to be a great support and friend throughout this journey.

When I received this particular diagnosis, I had no idea that I had any medical problem, certainly not cancer. I felt great and was leading a normal, active life, doing yard work, travelling, spending time with my husband, just enjoying life. Thinking back, I guess I should not have been too surprised by the diagnosis of breast cancer. My mother was diagnosed with breast cancer when she was 82 years old. She had a mastectomy and received no further treatment. She did not have a recurrence. My oldest sister was also diagnosed with breast cancer when she was 76 years old. She had a mastectomy, but did not require regular chemo or radiation. She did take a pill (hormone therapy) for 5 years and had no problems or recurrence.

It takes time to adjust to the fact that you have cancer— "that happens to someone else, not me." I recalled those I had known who had died because of cancer, who had suffered and had been very ill from the cancer and the chemotherapy treatments.

Dealing with cancer is not only a physical problem, but a mental problem as well. I was looking for understanding, encouragement, and, of course, a cure. It was a difficult time and I needed time to adjust and accept what was happening. Fortunately while going through all the scans and tests, I met many nurses and technicians who were very compassionate and gave me lots of encouragement.

Cancer is classified by stages (Stage I, II, III, IV), with Stage IV being the most serious. The stages are determined by size of tumor, lymph node involvement, and involvement of other organs. When all the tests and scans were finally completed, the doctor gave me the detailed diagnosis — Stage IV breast cancer that had metastasized and spread to some of the lymph glands, hip and spine. This is the type of diagnosis that is a death sentence. I asked my doctor what the prognosis looked like. He was reluctant to say, but I wanted to know. Based on other similar cases, he told me that history showed that I probably had 1- 2 years to live. While I was shocked, I had two thoughts. First, "I just got a reprieve — 1- 2 years was better than the 3 - 4 months I had been thinking about." Second, "I'm lucky, because many people don't get a warning and chance to prepare for death."

A doctor friend advised me not to place too much belief or concern in statistics. I was an individual and may react totally different than others. That gave me encouragement to keep a positive attitude. That simple comment from a friend made a huge impact on my life.

∿ Acceptance of Diagnosis ∿

Adjusting to and accepting the diagnosis was difficult and I was very anxious. The thought of cancer was a constant companion and never left me. I went to sleep thinking of it. If I woke during the night, it was my immediate thought. I literally felt like my life had been stolen from me and I wanted it back. It was all consuming—every thought, every minute of my life.

It was a difficult time for my family and me—lots of emotions, fear, anxiety and despair. Without our faith I don't know how we would have endured. Fortunately my family and friends were there for me. They all seemed to understand what I was going through and allowed me time to work through it. Their love and hugs helped a lot.

I couldn't run away from this—no matter where I went it hung over me like a heavy cloud. My daughter-in-law, Theresa, asked if I had a wish to take a trip or do something special (many people have special wishes when they know their life is coming to an end). There was nothing that I felt I needed to do that would make my life complete. I was perfectly happy where I was. I had my family, good neighbors, wonderful friends, a nice home, a great parish to support me spiritually, live in Florida with all its beauty—I didn't feel a need for anything more. But, I appreciated that she would think to ask me such a question.

Early on, I became very annoyed with the delay in starting treatment. I had always heard that early detection and getting treatment was important. Yet, it seemed that all we were doing was tests and more tests. It seemed to me that no one was in a hurry to get me started on a treatment. I realized later that all these tests were necessary to really learn what was going on in my body in order to offer the proper treatment. It was also necessary for my body to heal from the mastectomy before beginning chemo.

My oncologist explained to me that there was a possibility that I could participate in a clinical study. However, after we checked out all the details of the study, it was determined that I did not meet the requirements to participate in the study. Therefore, my oncologist determined the treatment that he thought would be best. Because the cancer was widespread, my only option for treatment was chemotherapy. With this treatment, we would try to keep the cancer from spreading, because it was unlikely that we could cure it.

So my chemo treatment began. It was in pill form and began in November 2006. This med was taken for two weeks followed by a week off from treatment and then the process started all over again. It was seven days before I began feeling any side effects. At first, I was thinking there was no problem with the treatment, that it was going to be an easy ride. However, it just took a little time for the drug to build in my body and I quickly found it to be quite unpleasant. This particular drug affected the nerve endings and caused lots of pain in my feet and hands. Gradually many other difficulties, including nausea, swollen lips, sore mouth, tiredness, among other things, began to show up. Each day was a new challenge while trying to deal with whatever came my way. I stayed on this treatment for two years

At one point I decided to get a "Handicap Parking" permit for my car. I didn't really want to do that, but since walking was becoming more difficult, it was needed and a blessing to have one.

I read spiritual books and scripture to help me accept this diagnosis. Psalm 40:2-3 seemed so appropriate at this time. *"I waited, waited for the Lord; Who bent down and heard my cry, Drew me out of the pit of destruction, out of the mud of the swamp, Set my feet upon rock, steadied my steps."*

⌣⁖ Journey of Faith ⁖⌣

My husband, Ray, was not in good health and was dealing with health problems of his own, including osteoporosis and early onset Alzheimers. There were lots of doctor visits for him in those days too. Fortunately, I was able to drive him to his appointments.

Because of his health condition Ray was unable to be with me for my doctor appointments and tests. While he had a very kind heart and was there for me, he could not be in the doctor's office with me. Hearing about my condition, the diagnosis and decisions directly from the doctor was just too taxing on his failing health. His heart began to race and he became physically ill. So, we agreed that he would ride with me to the visits, but stay in the waiting room and I would tell him about my visit when I came out. That worked well.

Even though this was very hard for him, my son, Mark, who lived nearby, accompanied me to these appointments. Mark was very thorough in understanding my medical condition, and built a good rapport with my doctor. It was always helpful to have another person hearing reports and asking questions. And, it was comforting to have him to lean on.

Prior to any procedure or surgery, Mark always offered me a simple, but meaningful, blessing. It gave me such assurance. He was always with me before each of my surgeries and before leaving the room, would bless me and make the "sign of the cross" on my forehead. He did the same each time I had my chemo treatments and continues this practice even now. When I travel and he drops me off at the airport, as he says farewell he places a sign of the cross on my forehead. This is a sign in the form of a cross as a prayer and sign of hope honoring God and asking for His blessing.

I was blessed with a very caring and understanding oncologist. Sadly, it is only when we have a need for the doctors that we come to really appreciate them. I respect and pray for this man, who faces very ill patients every day and gives them their unpleasant and sometimes devastating diagnosis. At the end of the day, when he goes home to his wife and children, it must be a challenge to switch off being doctor and becoming husband and father. How difficult that must be for him. We should always remember to pray for our doctors.

Shortly after my diagnosis, I met with my pastor, Father Tobin. He prayed with me and gave me the blessing for the sick — he was a wonderful support throughout this journey. He told me "Prayers are powerful, but always pray "Not my will but God's will". That was very difficult to do. I strongly wanted to be free of the cancer, but I did pray "not my will but God's will".

Once, Father Tobin asked me if I would be willing to come forward on a Sunday and allow the congregation to pray for me. I told him that I didn't think I could stand up in front of everyone in church—I was too emotional at that time. Sometime later, after reading about the power of healing prayer and understanding how important that could be, I agreed to come forward for prayers. It was an act of faith just to come forward and ask for prayer. During services, Father asked for those with a need for prayer, be it physical, emotional, mental or job related, to come forward. He led the congregation in prayer for the needs of all those standing before him. This was a beautiful and powerful prayer of intercession.

I knew that only prayer could get me through this difficult time in my life. So, I prayed, read spiritual books, and asked for and received the prayers of many people — people that I didn't even know. Along with the prayers from our parish, I had prayers from family, neighbors, friends, relatives, even my pharmacist. I attended Healing Prayer meetings and made a trip to Tallahassee to attend a Holy Spirit Seminar at my son, Ken's, parish and received more prayers there.

I've always believed that angels are God's special messengers and helpers. My favorite saint is St Padre Pio, so I turned to him for his intercession. During his lifetime, he always had his angel delivering messages for him. Knowing that my guardian angel is a special messenger that would carry my petitions to God, I began giving my prayers and petitions to my guardian angel for delivery directly to God. Every day I asked for healing. This was very comforting to me to know I had this special help line.

Exodus 24:20 reminds us of this special gift that God has given us. *"See I am sending an angel before you, to guard you on the way and bring you to the place I have prepared."*

There were many doctor visits and medical tests along the way, and I tried to turn these times into prayer time. Some of the scans required about 1½ hours, so I would use that time to do spiritual reading and praying. When I had to lie quietly for long periods of time for a scan, I would silently sing songs of praise to God in my mind and heart. *"Praise God, Praise God, Alleluia!"* The time passed very easily and quickly, and I was able to accept these challenges. Luke 11:9-10 gave me encouragement and confidence that there is a greater power to draw on. *"And I tell you, ask and you will receive; seek and you will find; knock and the door will be opened to you. For everyone who asks, receives; and the one who seeks, finds; and to the one who knocks, the door will be opened."*

My activities were often limited, but as long as I wasn't nauseated I thought I could deal with it. I felt like the Lord prompted me to offer this challenge as a prayer for the souls in Purgatory. It just seemed like the right thing to do.

As the chemo treatments continued and my faith continued to grow, I was confident that my next scan would show that I was completely clear of cancer. I made a commitment to God that I would come forward and speak of his love, kindness and power to as many people as possible.

In August 2007, Father Tobin asked me to speak at all the church services on a weekend to tell how God had worked in my life and of the spiritual journey I was on. It was an opportunity to tell how God guided me to turn a very difficult challenge into a time of prayer and faith. Even though I was uncertain of the cancer status at that time, I really felt I would soon be cancer free. After speaking, a number of people told me that hearing my testimonial gave them courage, and helped them through a difficult time to place their trust in God.

It became apparent that a battle with cancer is like a marathon, requiring time, effort and endurance. This would be a marathon, not a sprint. As we talked to my doctor about treatment I asked if there was a possibility of a cure. Since it was in the bone, my oncologist said his goal would be to keep it from spreading. He told me that during his years of treating cancer patients he had only had one person with a similar condition who showed no further sign of cancer, and he considered that to be a miracle. I told him that was exactly what I was praying for.

Many patients research each drug and question every test and result. I decided to let the doctor handle the meds and treatment, just do his job. Since I felt I was not a doctor, it was better for me to be a good patient. However, not everyone feels that way. Each person needs to deal with their treatments in their own way. What works for one person may not work for someone else.

I told my doctor that I didn't want, or feel the need for, all the details of my cancer or treatment. If there was anything I needed to know, he should tell me. If I wanted to know more details, I would ask. I wanted to concentrate on getting well and keeping a positive attitude.

A petscan the following December still showed some cancer. It was diminishing, but still present. I really thought it would be completely gone by that time, but again, there was a lesson for me here—I needed to be patient. I continued receiving chemo treatment and still felt I was receiving a miracle. It just wasn't exactly the way I had asked for it—it was God's way.

༶ INCREASING FAITH ༷

The doctors were certain of their original diagnosis of Stage IV cancer. The tests had been conclusive beyond any doubt. The goal of my chemo regimen was to buy me some time, but nothing more. But, one day it came to me that God is all powerful and, if it would be good for me, He could heal me with no problem, regardless of my diagnosis. It was like turning on a light bulb. I had just realized that if it was God's will and I believed it, I would be cured. What a relief! I had a feeling of total peace after that. Totally surrendering my illness to God allowed me to be at peace knowing and believing everything would be OK. I just had to be open to receiving His gift.

Mark 11:24 says *"Therefore I tell you, all that you ask for in prayer, believe that you will receive it and it shall be yours."* Matthew 17:20 says *"Amen, I say to you, if you have faith the size of a mustard seed, you will say to this mountain "Move from here to there and it will move. Nothing will be impossible for you."*

That was the way my faith for a cure began—about the size of a mustard seed. Gradually, and slowly, that faith grew larger and larger. When I prayed about being healed, and thanking God for my healing, a voice in the back of my head would say, "Healing can't happen. You will not get a good report. Remember what the doctor said. You cannot be healed." I recognized that it was the devil attempting to destroy my faith. Each time, I would say, "No" and continue to pray. Renouncing Satan's lies became a regular part of my life.

Again the Psalms gave me courage to continue this battle. *"Psalm 23:4 "Even when I walk through a dark valley, I fear no harm for you are at my side; your rod and staff give me courage."*

One day while I was praying, I actually found myself thanking God for allowing this illness in my life. When I realized what I was saying it startled me. But, I continued the prayer, knowing that God had blessed me greatly and would take care of me. I had total peace and acceptance. This illness made me stop and realize what is really important in life, i.e. faith in God, family and friends.

In July 2008 another scan showed cancer cells in my right hip along with a weakened femur bone and hip. The doctors thought it was caused by the cancer and chemo treatment. They determined that it would be wise to have a pin put in the thigh and hip to avoid a possible break. I had the surgery and that proved to be another chance to tell others of God's blessings.

On the day of surgery the schedule was delayed and I had to wait in pre-op for an extended time. The nurses came in about every ten minutes and asked if I needed some medication to help me relax because of the wait. I refused the meds. I had prayed for the doctor and medical staff and placed my life and surgery in God's hands. I didn't have to worry about it—and I didn't. One nurse was very interested in how I had accepted my earlier cancer diagnosis. I took the opportunity to share my story with her.

During my time in the hospital, the lady in the next bed was having some major family problems as well as health problems. I encouraged her to pray and have confidence that God would see her through if she just asked Him. So again my health problem provided an opportunity to share with others and encourage them to place their trust in God during difficult times.

The surgery that day went well and there were no complications. Time and therapy were required to recuperate.

⌒: A Difficult Time :⌒

By October 2008 the pill form chemo treatment I had been receiving was no longer effective. The doctors decided to change the drug regimen, and also the delivery method. The medicine would be administered via IV. My treatment and evaluation of my condition took on new meaning by this time. I had survived two years. I was moving beyond the time the doctors had given me. I was on God's clock now! It gave me new hope.

Each time I received my treatment I said a prayer over the medicine and IV injection site, asking for a successful treatment and cure. My body has never tolerated medications very well and my body certainly did NOT like this new treatment. I suffered through days with an elevated temperature, bowel problems, exhaustion, mouth sores, headaches and weakness. All of this became a part of life. On the morning of the 33rd day after starting this IV chemo regimen, I found my pillow covered with hair. I was losing my hair, and quickly. So, I had my head shaved and didn't have to think about hair styles for a while. Scarves and wigs became my new friends.

This also presented some concern. Wearing a scarf or hat usually indicated a cancer patient. I didn't want to tell the world that I had cancer or be treated differently because I had cancer. It was like putting a "C" on my forehead. After a bit I was able to adjust my thinking and decided that it was no big deal. I wasn't alone in this, many others go through this, and I needed to accept this as something that would eventually pass.

Though all these conditions were presenting problems, I continued to focus on the end result, knowing all these difficulties would eventually end and I would feel better and life would get back to normal.

The schedule for receiving the IV chemo was once per week for 3 weeks followed by 1 week off. This schedule and meds continued until April 2009. Receiving these treatments was a rather interesting experience. The infusion center was the place all the cancer patients came for treatment. The room was lined with lounge chairs. Patients sat here to receive the IV chemo treatments. Actually, we all took our naps here. One of the meds a patient receives is benadryl to help avoid reactions to the chemo drug. By the time the chemo started, the patient was nearly in "lala" land. Mark always took me to the treatments and waited with me until he was sure everything was going well. He and I laughed about how all of a sudden I was sleeping and he would leave for a while.

St Padre Pio said that Jesus spoke to him regarding his own suffering. Jesus suggested to him that we sometimes need to suffer so that we remember the need for God in our life. After reading that, I thought it may be why God was giving me new challenges periodically. It reminded me of His power and love, and how much I need Him in my life. Each new challenge is a sign of God's love—even when it is difficult to accept.

It seemed that each new cancer drug offered the possibility of hope, but also the possibility of death. In April 2009 I started a new drug for treatment. Immediately there were serious side effects, including a dangerously low blood count. One evening I had to go to the ER and was immediately hospitalized. In what seemed like just a few hours, my condition deteriorated rapidly and I developed pneumonia. I was moved to Intensive Care, where I spent nine days on a ventilator. My condition was touch and go for a while, but I eventually improved to the point where the doctors thought I could breathe on my own.

However, it didn't last long and I spent another week on a CPAP. That is a machine with a mask that assists with breathing, but does not require a tube down the throat. I also developed a serious intestinal bacterial infection known as C-difficile. On two different occasions during that time in the hospital, my condition was so serious the doctors told my family that they didn't think I would survive.

There was a wonderful and knowledgeable staff of doctors who saw me through this difficult time. The hospital staff was also remarkable, dedicated and caring.

The mind is definitely affected by meds and I was heavily medicated for a significant period of time. During that time, I do remember having what I can only describe as hallucinations. My mind seemed to connect some real event with thoughts that had no basis in reality. At one time, I remember that I could hear piano music. For a long time, I thought this was just some crazy thought. Later I learned that there was a player piano in a lobby area near my room and I must have been hearing it. Most of my thoughts were not so pleasant. I remember at one point that the entire hospital staff was preparing for Christmas. Never mind that it was actually April. The staff was so busy decorating the hospital for the holidays that they completely forgot to take care of me. Thank goodness that the hospital didn't ask me to complete a patient care survey when I was discharged. That would have been very embarrassing.

And then there was the time it seemed we were next to a carnival and I could hear the calliope. One of the weirdest memories was the time when I thought all my family and grandchildren were there, but no one would come to talk to me. They stayed in the next room. I do recall a day that I prayed that God would take me home. I felt so bad and I was so tired. But He had other plans.

My son, Mark, related an incident that occurred during my illness. When I was on CPAP, my condition worsened and it looked like I was not going to make it. The Minister of the Sick from our church brought the Eucharist, but the nurses told her I could not receive because of my condition. As the minister walked off, Mark went after her and brought her back. He told her that I needed the Eucharist more than anything that the doctors or hospital had to offer. Mark told the staff that he would take full responsibility, and then proceeded to remove the breathing machine for just a moment. The minister placed just a small piece of the Eucharist on my tongue, and then Mark placed the mask back on my face. But God is so great that even the tiniest bit of Jesus is "more than enough." That day I experienced my own Eucharistic miracle. Beginning then, my tenuous condition stabilized, and slowly, but surely, began to improve. Psalm 145:3 states my feeling so well— *"Great is the Lord and worthy of high praise; God's grandeur is beyond understanding."*

As it turned out, the enemy that I fought during that month in the hospital was not Stage IV cancer. It was the cure that almost killed me. My body had reacted poorly to the new chemo medication. I came to understand firsthand what people meant when they said that the goal is for the chemo to kill the cancer before it kills you. Death had knocked on my door, but God had once again rescued me.

It is a difficult task for medical staff to care for someone in my condition. I was in ICU for several weeks, and the issues that threatened my health varied during that time. I guess I was kind of a moving target. Mark's dedication during this time was so important. I couldn't speak for myself, so his commitment to explain my condition to the constantly rotating medical staff was a critical factor in my recovery.

Other than my hallucinations, my memory of that month is nonexistent. It was strange and difficult to comprehend. I didn't remember the initial incident of going to the ER, and only remembered about the last week in the hospital. When I finally became aware of my surroundings, I was very weak and unable to feed myself. Mark came to the hospital each day to feed me breakfast, brought me my favorite cup of cappuccino, and began to relate to me what had happened during that time.

By the time I was able to get out of bed, I had been off my feet for almost a month. To say that I was weak would be an understatement. So the first time out of bed with a therapist was a big event. I was able to take about four steps. Quite an accomplishment. After being so near to death, this small thing was an occasion to rejoice. Oh, the appreciation I had for such a simple thing as standing upright. It's these small things that take on new meaning and appreciation after being so near death.

I thought that my memory would eventually return, but that never happened. When I asked my doctor about my lack of memory, he said I should just be grateful that I was alive and not concern myself with all the details. I think he is right—sometimes ignorance is bliss. After spending a month in the hospital and another 1½ weeks in rehab I finally went home to recuperate.

It was sometime later before I had the strength to venture out. The first Sunday I was able to attend church Father Tobin was outside shaking hands of parishioners. When I walked up to him he hugged me and said "Here's Lazarus—back from the dead". We had a good laugh over that. Thankfully, we had kept our sense of humor through it all.

As my health was improving, sadly, Ray's health was deteriorating. Thankfully, I was soon able to drive again and take him to his appointments. He had not been driving for several years.

ᨹᨷ MORE CHALLENGES ᨷᨻ

During a subsequent doctor's appointment my doctor commented about all the prayers I received while in the hospital. (My family was praying at my bedside constantly.) He went on to say how "sometimes there is no explanation for things that happen to patients—doctors and medicine don't always have the answer—there is a greater power." Then he added "With all that you've been through and have survived so much, I think you fall into the category of a miracle." I thanked him and said "It's the power of prayer."

My doctor made a statement that we seldom hear. He said that usually doctors think they have the answers for treating patients — they have the education, experience and know about all the drugs. However, sometimes they have to admit that there is a higher power who is in charge. I had to agree with that statement.

As time went on, even though I was not receiving any chemo or other treatment, tests showed that the cancer had diminished. It was obvious to me that God was curing my cancer.

In January 2010 I was diagnosed with pneumonia again. I was stronger this time and with the help of medication I was able to overcome it and avoid hospitalization. In April I developed swelling in my right arm. My right breast and lymph glands had been removed previously. Therefore, lymph could not flow easily through the arm. This caused a build-up of fluid in the arm causing swelling, known as lymphedema. This is not uncommon, and can be painful at times and limit activities. I received therapy and started wearing an elastic sleeve on the arm to limit the swelling. This is a condition that will have its challenges, but I can deal with that.

In May 2010 it appeared as if the only remaining cancer was in a lymph gland below my right arm. By removing it and following that with some radiation, the doctors thought I could become cancer free. So I had the surgery and 25 radiation treatments.

As I was starting radiation therapy, I somehow pulled the ligament in my left arm, which was quite painful. During the treatments, I had to lie very quietly with my arms above my head. While my right side was fine, the left arm with the pulled ligament was very painful.

As had become my practice, at the beginning of each treatment I asked for God's blessing—to allow the equipment to work well to kill all the bad cells in my body, and to allow the healthy cells to flourish. I silently sang praise to God for all his blessings. I thanked him for those who made the equipment, technicians, doctors and everyone involved. There were times I thought I could not stand the pain in my arm, but then I would say to myself that this was nothing compared to what Christ suffered on the cross.

All the radiation was completed, and no further treatments were planned. For the near future, I would continue to be monitored by my doctor.

By this time Ray's health had deteriorated considerably. His osteoporosis kept him in almost constant pain. He was also experiencing the effects of Alzheimers, making it a very difficult time for him. He was hospitalized in November 2010. From the hospital he went to rehab and then a nursing home. Unfortunately, he needed more care than I could give him at home. His health deteriorated rapidly and he died in January 2011.

ᴍ My Second Chance ᴥ

Almost miraculously, my health continued to improve, so my doctor continued to keep me in a monitoring status. He was reluctant to give me more chemo, because of my serious reactions. My meds for the future would be "Prayers".

During my journey, I developed my own personal devotion. It helped me connect with God and rest in His grace. Every day I make the sign of the cross over each area of my body where I've had cancer cells and pray "In the name of Jesus I thank you for healing this part of my body—for removing all cancer cells and allowing only healthy cells to grow in my body." I also pray "Dear God, you have healed me and for this I am grateful. Let me know what you wish me to do for having received this special blessing. My life is in your hands and I will serve you in whatever way you desire. Amen".

In August 2012 I had a routine appointment with my oncologist. Lymphedema in my right arm was causing it to swell and was painful. My doctor thought there may be some cancer activity in the right arm area and ordered a petscan. The results of the scan were astounding –no cancer anywhere in my body! My doctor stated, "No cancer present, and we cannot explain why." I told him I knew why, that I'd been seeking a miracle ever since the time of diagnosis and God had given me a miracle. The lymphedema cannot be cured (of course that's also what they said about the cancer), so I will need to live with it unless Jesus cures it too. My thought is that God is probably saying "Look I gave you a miracle and removed the cancer, and now you are complaining about a swollen arm." So, I'll accept it as a daily reminder to say "Thanks" for blessings received.

Among all the other medical issues, I've had a dangerously low blood count for a long time. Our bone marrow produces the blood that flows through our bodies and there is nothing that can be done to improve the body's ability to produce blood. If my blood count should become a problem, a blood transfusion may be necessary. However, over the last couple of years, my chronically low blood levels have improved, much to the doctor's surprise. God is good.

The visits to my oncologist are not as frequent now. God continues his blessings in His time. A June 2013 blood test showed my blood counts all in normal range. My doctor cannot explain it and doesn't know why. I told him I know why—it's the power of prayer and God still working his miracle.

So many thoughts ran through my mind when I was first facing cancer, and the possibility of death. I found that it was necessary to wrap my arms around the situation and understand what was happening to me. I had to come to a point of acceptance. There was no quick fix, no wishing the reality of it away. I had no control over what would happen in the future. The only thing I could control was the present and I had to decide if I would live each day in hope and in a positive manner, or live it in despair and misery.

Through the process of reading numerous books, I've come to realize a few important things in my life. I needed to count my blessings. God had been good to me and I needed to be grateful. Often we don't remember to say "Thanks" until something tragic comes along. So I began to be grateful for each day that I had and began asking for healing. I found that I had to actually believe in God's goodness and willingness to heal me. Too often we don't believe we can be healed. We ask for healing, but don't truly believe it will happen.

It doesn't mean that I don't go to the doctor and don't take my medicine. I believe that God uses the nurses and doctors as his instruments of healing. It's just important that we accept what has been sent to us and deal with it in a positive way.

Never let anyone or anything convince you to give up the fight. Attitude is critical in the battles we face in life, be it cancer, or any other disease or challenge. Positive attitude and hope give us courage. It's like sunshine on a cloudy day.

It was six years from my diagnosis of Stage IV cancer to being "Free of Cancer." I was blessed during difficult challenges and experienced an amazing journey of faith and healing. I have grown close to God and live at peace. God has been good to me and I will be forever thankful.

Even though the cancer, chemo and radiation have taken a toll on my body, I will live my life as fully as possible. I will accept the challenges that still lie before me, and I will praise God for the great blessing He has given me.

I have received a **second chance** at life. My days are now spent actively participating in various organizations, doing volunteer work, taking music lessons and spending time with family and friends. Each day is a gift from God and I'm enjoying every one of them.

My prayer of thanks will always be:

Psalm 92:2-3

It is good to give thanks to the Lord,
     to sing praise to your name, Most High
To proclaim your love in the morning,
     your faithfulness in the night.

༈ Acknowledgements ༈

- A special thanks goes to my oncologist and all the doctors who cared for me during this time. They were compassionate, dedicated, knowledgeable, and wonderful to my family and me. I believe that God guided them and used them as His instruments to do His work.

- My son, Mark, designed and created the cover of this book. My son, Ken, edited and helped me to put my thoughts into words. Bob Schuchts, a family friend, took time from his busy schedule to write the Foreword. Their help, support and encouragement are greatly appreciated. A job well done by each of them.

- Many people have been encouraging me to write my story. I delayed a long time, but reached the conclusion that this may be the reason God has healed me—that I should make others aware of His healing power. Therefore, I offer thanks and appreciation to all those who encouraged me to write "Second Chance".

– This witness is not about me, it is about the goodness and blessings of God. I do not take credit for anything; in His mercy, God blessed me. While this is about my journey through cancer treatment, I believe this can be applied to any disease or challenge we have in life. It is a matter of offering to God each challenge in our life, knowing that He will walk the journey with us and will never leave us.

We need to stop wanting and begin believing—that's when God's power takes over.

PRAISE GOD!!!!
Psalm 13:6
I trust in your faithfulness.
Grant my heart joy in your help,
That I may sing of the Lord,
"How good our God has been to me!"

᪣ Favorite Prayers ᪢

MY PRAYER FOR MONDAY
(By Father John Mulligan, SM)

My Lord God,
I do not see the road ahead of me.
I cannot know for certain
Where it will end...

I know that You will lead me
By the right road,
Though I may know nothing about it.
Therefore I trust You always.
I will not fear,
For You are with me,
And You will never leave me
To face my perils alone.

BLESS ME LORD

Your healing power is needed
Extend your hand to me,
Undeserving though I am
Your love will set me free.

You know my every action
My thoughts and wishes too,
Please answer when I seek your help
For all healing comes from you!

PRAYER FOR THOSE AFFECTED BY CANCER
(From prayer card by Missionary
Oblates of Mary Immaculate)

Might God,
Send your loving angels to those
whose lives are affected by cancer.
Give them strength.
Give them faith.
Give them hope.
Help them to realize
That wherever this road
May lead them,
It will be less difficult in the company
of those they love.
May they never forget that each day
is a precious gift fromYou.
Amen.

PRAYER IN TIME OF NEED
(By the Marianist Mission)

I am hurting dear Lord,
I ask You to listen to the cry of my heart.
Strengthen my faith
and give me patience to bear my trouble.
Visit me with your grace.
I leave all my cares to Your wisdom, love,
understanding, and goodness. Amen

THE OBLATE PRAYER
(From prayer card by Missionary
Oblates of Mary Immaculate)

My God, I give you this day,
I offer you all the good that I will do in it.
And, I promise to accept all the difficulties
I may meet therein with love for you.

PRAYER FOR MEDICATION

Dear God,
Please bless this area of my arm where the medicine enters
my body. Let all the equipment work properly to allow the
medicine to flow freely though the veins so problems will
not occur. May this medicine rid my body of all cancer cells
and illness and bring total healing to my body. I ask this in
Jesus name. Amen

JEREMIAH 18:14

Heal me, Lord, that I may be healed;
Save me, that I may be saved,
For it is you whom I praise.

MY SPECIAL PRAYER OF THANKS

(Make the sign of the cross over each area of the body where cancer cells have been and pray:)
In the name of Jesus I thank you for healing this part of my body—for removing all cancer cells and allowing only healthy cells to grow in my body.
Dear God, you have healed me and for this I am grateful. Let me know what you wish me to do for having received this special blessing. My life is in your hands and I will serve you in whatever way you desire. Amen.

Psalm 92:2-3
It is good to give thanks to the Lord,
   to sing praise to your name, Most High
To proclaim your love in the morning,
   your faithfulness in the night.

Psalm 13:6
I trust in your faithfulness.
Grant my heart joy in your help,
That I may sing of the Lord,
"How good our God has been to me!"

PRAISE GOD!!!!

44

WHEN CANCER PAYS A VISIT

- Never give up

- Life is a gift from God—live it to the fullest

- Keep a positive attitude

- Think about happy experiences

- Enjoy each day, even when not feeling great

- Remember to pray, God is always listening

- Don't try to be doctor and patient; just be a good patient

- Someone else is always worse off

- Remember to laugh

- Have some fun

- Keep an attitude of gratitude

- Have a sense of humor

- Count blessings

Made in the USA
Lexington, KY
25 July 2014